RAILWAYS OF THE WEST OF ENGLAND IN THE 1980s

Kevin Redwood

AMBERLEY

First published 2019

Amberley Publishing
The Hill, Stroud
Gloucestershire, GL5 4EP

www.amberley-books.com

ISBN 978 1 4456 8917 3 (print)
ISBN 978 1 4456 8918 0 (ebook)

British Library Cataloguing in Publication Data.
A catalogue record for this book is available from the British Library.

Typesetting by Aura Technology and Software Services, India. Printed in UK.

Introduction

The Western Region of British Rail was split into three operating divisions: the London Division, the South Wales Division and the West of England Division. The West of England Division was the largest of the three and stretched from the regional boundary with the London Midland Region at Barnt Green (to the north of Bromsgrove), all the way down to Penzance, some 286 route miles away. The photographs in this book were taken between 1980 and 1988 and show a varied selection of locations from across the West of England Division.

Bristol was the centre of the division in more ways than one. The divisional headquarters were located in the Bristol & Exeter Building, which stands adjacent to Bristol Temple Meads station and had formerly been offices of the Bristol & Exeter Railway. Bristol Temple Meads was also the most important station in the West of England.

Across the region in the 1980s were a number of important railway locations, each differing in character. Worcester in the north still retained semaphore signalling and was the hub of a network of DMU services as well as loco-hauled services to Paddington via the Cotswolds. Gloucester saw a lot of passing traffic while a number of trains called to reverse and change locos. At Swindon the BREL Works was an important employer in the town, until it closed in 1986. Bristol was the main hub of the division with inter-city services to Paddington, and on the cross-country route, and also seeing Portsmouth to Cardiff trains. Westbury had seen a huge rise in stone traffic from the Mendip quarries during the 1970s. In Devon the station at Exeter St Davids remained busy with inter-city services, trains from Waterloo and DMUs working local branch trains. Plymouth was the originating point for many inter-city services while Laira depot maintained a fleet of HST locos and DMUs. In Cornwall, St Blazey was the centre for the freight traffic in the area. At the end of the line at Penzance, the depot at Long Rock serviced HSTs for Paddington and cross-country services.

The two principle loco depots on the division were at Bristol Bath Road and Plymouth Laira, and each had an allocation of HSTs, locos and DMUs. Smaller depots at Gloucester, Swindon, Newton Abbot, St Blazey and Penzance each had a small allocation of Class 08 shunters for work in their local area.

Bath Road depot in Bristol had an allocation of over ninety locos at the start of the decade. Although a pair of Class 03 shunters had been transferred away in 1980, over a dozen Class 08s were allocated and these were employed in and around Bristol as well as at Westbury and Taunton. The Class 31s were employed on a mix of passenger and parcels services as well as freight and engineers workings. The Class 47 fleet was found on all types of work while the Class 37s and Class 56s were mostly used on aggregate trains. The Bristol-based DMU fleet were identified by a 'B' prefix to the allocated set number and included Class 101, 117, 118, 119, 120 and 121s. The DMU fleet was normally fuelled and maintained at Marsh Junction, and worked over a wide area, to Cardiff, Worcester, Weymouth and Taunton. St Phillips Marsh HST depot had fourteen sets allocated for services to Paddington.

Plymouth Laira depot also had a large allocation of around fifty locos at the start of the 1980s. The Class 08 fleet shunted yards in the Plymouth area, and in 1981 was augmented by the Newton Abbot allocation when that depot closed. The small fleet of Class 25s that had been carrying out local freight and passenger work in Devon and Cornwall was transferred away in 1980 to be replaced by Class 37s. The depot allocation of Class 47s undertook a wide variety of duties, while Laira's Class 50 fleet worked on the cross-country route as well as the Waterloo to Exeter services. The Plymouth-based DMU fleet was identified by the set prefix 'P' and included Class 118, 120 and 121 sets, though the Class 120 sets were soon transferred away, and later Class 108 and 122 sets came in as replacements. The DMU fleet worked mostly on the branch lines of Devon and Cornwall, and were not normally seen east of Exeter. Laira depot serviced and maintained HST sets and the cross-country HST fleet was based there.

Five smaller loco depots on the division each had an allocation of Class 08 shunting locos for local work in their area, though some of these depots were closed or lost their allocation during the 1980s. In 1980 Gloucester Horton Road depot had eight Class 08s allocated to shunt in Gloucester and Worcester, but by 1986 reduced workload meant the allocation had dropped to four Class 08s. The Class 08 allocation at Swindon was principally to shunt in the BREL Swindon Works and local yards. There had been seven locos based at Swindon in 1980, but by the time the BREL works closed in 1986 the fleet had dwindled to three locos. Newton Abbot depot closed in 1981, but prior to that there had been an allocation of seven Class 08s. These had worked at Newton Abbot and Exeter, while one was outbased at Meldon Quarry. St Blazey had three locos, one of which worked a local freight trip on weekdays to Wenford Bridge. Finally, there was a pair of Class 08s at Penzance, which worked at the station and Long Rock depot.

The most important passenger services on the West of England Division were those from Paddington to Bristol, the West Country and the Cotswolds. These were mostly worked by HSTs though some peak hours services were still worked by loco and coaches. Cross-country services were also mostly in the hands of HST sets but again there were a number of loco and coaches workings. On summer Saturdays the situation was very different, with many additional trains running to Paignton, Plymouth and Penzance. Newquay also saw an increased service in the summer, where the normal winter service of seven daily branch trains was supplemented by through services to Manchester, Newcastle and Paddington. Many of these additional summer Saturday trains were worked by locos not fitted with train heating equipment and which were normally confined to freight-only work in the winter. This could bring unusual visitors to the West Country. Other loco and coaches workings were found on the Portsmouth

Harbour to Bristol and Cardiff route, which had increased from a poor two-hourly service hauled by Class 31/4s in 1980 to an hourly service worked by Southern Region Class 33s. Most branch services were worked by DMUs.

Freight traffic varied across the division, although most local freight depots had already closed by the start of the decade. In the north of the division there was significant traffic from South Wales to the Midlands and the North. In the Bristol and Avonmouth area there were a number of important freight terminals, while the two major Mendip quarries at Merehead and Whatley produced a huge tonnage of stone traffic. In the West Country the movement of clay was important, both for export via Fowey and Dover, and for domestic customers across the BR network. At the start of the 1980s the traditional vacuum-braked wagon-load network was in decline, but locations like Gloucester New Yard, Bristol Kingsland Road and Exeter Riverside Yard were still busy. By 1984 the vacuum-braked network was closed down as remaining freight was transferred to the new air-braked Speedlink network. Feeder services from St Blazey and Eastleigh then connected into the Speedlink network at Severn Tunnel Junction, which offered overnight connections across BR.

During the 1980s much of the remaining traditional semaphore signalling was being replaced as new power signal boxes opened at Westbury and Exeter. The new Westbury panel opened in 1984 and by 1985 controlled the route as far as Somerton, while the Exeter panel opened in 1985 and by 1987 had extended control from Somerton to Totnes.

I was born in Exeter into a railway family, within sight and sound of Exmouth Junction. As a child, my mother, Ruth, would take me in my pushchair to watch the shunting taking place there and this helped to form my fascination with trains. She has had to put up with me talking about railways ever since. My late father, Norman Redwood, worked for the WR civil engineers as a wagon inspector so I learned much about the engineer's wagon fleet, and I sometimes accompanied him on visits to yards and depots. Most of the photos in this book were taken between 1980 and 1985, when I was working as a TOPS clerk in the Bristol Area Freight Centre. I usually travelled alone, but on a number of trips I went with my friend and BR colleague Roland Carp, who did the driving. I must also thank my partner Antoinette for her support as I worked on this book, and for indulging my interest in trains.

In the early 1980s most passenger services serving Worcester were worked by DMUs, the usual exceptions being some of the Paddington services, which were normally worked by Class 50s. On 31 July 1983, the unusual arrival of Class 56 No. 56033 brought some variety. The White Rose Rambler (organised by F&W Railtours) had departed Plymouth at 05.50 and called for a photographic stop at Worcester Shrub Hill on the way to Yorkshire.

A quiet scene at Worcester Shrub Hill on 12 February 1982 with a Class 117 Pressed Steel set in the platform. DMUs from WR depots at Bristol, Cardiff and Reading as well as LMR sets from Tyseley were all regular visitors. Reading-based set L419, formed of Nos 51356, 59508 and 51398, had recently arrived on a service from Hereford.

By the early 1980s, and apart from the Metal Box factory to the south of the station, there was little revenue-earning freight traffic loaded or unloaded in Worcester. However, the yard adjacent to the station was busy at times with civil engineers traffic. On 12 February 1982, Gloucester-allocated No. 08778 shunts a rake of grampus wagons. In the background are some new seacow ballast hoppers wearing the recently introduced 'Dutch' livery.

Midland Region DMUs based at Tyseley were sometimes seen in Gloucester. A Tyseley-allocated Class 101 Metro-Cammell DMU formed of Nos 53310, 59128 and 53326 arrives at Gloucester on 4 September 1984 and is seen passing Horton Road depot.

In 1980 Gloucester Horton Road depot had an allocation of eight Class 08 shunting locos, two of which, Nos 08778 and 08836, are seen at the depot on 6 November 1980. As well as supplying locos for freight trains from nearby Gloucester New Yard, a number of parcels trains were also re-engined at Gloucester, meaning locos from many depots could be seen at Horton Road. On shed are Nos 47128 (Cardiff Canton), 20176 and 20070 (Toton), 47026 (Laira), 25197 (Bescot) and 31296 (Old Oak Common).

Arriving at Gloucester on 10 July 1985 behind No. 37206 is the 15.42 Swindon to Gloucester service. The train is formed of failed Cardiff-allocated Class 101 Metro-Cammell set C823 comprising vehicle Nos 51505, 59082 and 51511. After reversal the same combination worked out on the 16.50 service to Weston-super-Mare. This platform, which had been extended in 1977, was one of the longest on the network and measured 1,977 feet in length.

Following closure of Gloucester Eastgate station, passenger services from the south that called at Gloucester were required to reverse before heading north towards Cheltenham and Birmingham. With loco-hauled services this sometimes also included a change of loco. On 10 July 1985 No. 47553 brings the 16.25 Paddington to Cheltenham into Gloucester, where Toton-allocated No. 45131 was waiting to work the train forward on the final leg of the journey to Cheltenham.

In 1975 the former Midland Railway station Gloucester Eastgate was closed, with all passenger services being concentrated on the former GWR station at Gloucester Central, which was subsequently renamed simply Gloucester. On 4 September 1984 Toton's No. 45139 is seen at Gloucester with an empty stock working from Cardiff. Platform 4, behind the train, had only been brought back into passenger use earlier in 1984.

Local services from Gloucester to Worcester, Swindon, Bristol and Cardiff were mostly worked by DMUs based at either Bristol or Cardiff. Here, two DMU sets are seen at Gloucester on 4 September 1984. On the left, Bristol-based Class 117 Pressed Steel set B428 formed of vehicles Nos 51366, 59518 and 51408 is waiting to depart for Swindon. On the right, Cardiff-based Class 101 Metro-Cammell set C822 formed of vehicle Nos 51495, 59096 and 51510 is working the 13.05 service from Swindon to Worcester Foregate Street.

Bristol Temple Meads was the hub of a number of travelling post office (TPO) services. One service that ran for many years was 1E38, the 19.35 Bristol Temple Meads to Newcastle, and which formerly also conveyed passenger accommodation. At Gloucester the shunter is about to uncouple No. 45101, which worked 1E38 up from Bristol on the evening of 10 July 1985.

The North Sidings adjacent to Swindon station were often filled with DMUs or coaching stock from other regions that were en route to or from Swindon Works. On this occasion on 4 September 1984 a Swindon-built Western Region Class 120 set is stabled in the North Sidings. Cardiff-allocated set C615 is formed of vehicles Nos 51781, 59682 and 51788, and is fitted with headlights for working over the Central Wales line.

During the 1980s Swindon station comprised a single island with platform facing each side as well as a west-facing bay from which local services departed. On the Down side of the main lines there was a separate parcels platform. Cardiff-allocated Metro-Cammell set C822 formed of vehicles Nos 51495, 59096 and 51510 waits to depart from the bay platform as the 13.05 service to Worcester Foregate Street on 4 September 1984.

A view looking west from the platform at Swindon on 4 September 1984 as the 11.00 Paddington to Swansea HST service departs. A Pressed Steel Class 117 DMU, set B428, formed of vehicles 51366, 59518 and 51408, approaches the bay platform. Stabled in the loco depot is No. 37280, while in the distance in the West Loop is a Speedlink working for Ripple Lane headed by No. 47314.

Approaching Platform 3 at Swindon on 4 September 1984 is a Paddington-bound HST headed by power car No. 43002 *Top of the Pops*. The power car had been named only a few days earlier, on 30 August 1984, in a ceremony at Bristol Temple Meads.

The depot at Swindon had a small allocation of Class 08 shunters for shunting in the BREL Works and yards in Swindon. Standing outside the single road shed is No. 08523, which had been a Tinsley-allocated loco, and behind it is Metropolitan-Vickers Class 28 Co-Bo No. 5705. The Class 37s stabled alongside are Nos 37280 and 37255 and the date is 4 September 1984.

A view of the east end of Stoke Gifford on 7 September 1983 with Bristol Parkway station in the distance. Standing on the Up loop is No. 47088 *Samson,* waiting to work the 08.55 trip to the ARC quarry at Tytherington. The train is formed of empty PGA hoppers going for repair at Tytherington and a set of ten empty sealion hoppers to load ballast for the Southern Region. This was one of up to six trips that ran over the branch each weekday.

The marshalling yards at Stoke Gifford closed in 1971 and much of the site of the former Up yard was used for the car park of Bristol Parkway station. However, the Down yard was later brought back into use for stone traffic from ARC Tytherington and subsequently also carried out local marshalling of Speedlink traffic for the Bristol and Avonmouth area. On 10 July 1985 No. 47376 waits in the Down yard with T78 Speedlink trip for Hallen Marsh.

At Stoke Gifford Junction there are routes to Bristol, Hallen Marsh (including access to Stoke Gifford Tip) and South Wales. The 08.43 Swansea to Paddington service comes over Stoke Gifford Junction on the approach to Bristol Parkway on 10 July 1985.

The Severn Beach branch service from Bristol Temple Meads called at nine intermediate stations in north Bristol and the Avonmouth area. Bristol-allocated single power cars worked many of the services but at peak times three-car DMUs were also used. On 5 October 1983 the 09.05 service from Severn Beach to Bristol Temple Meads is seen at Hallen Marsh, being worked by Class 117 Pressed Steel set B437 (formed of vehicles Nos 51338, 59504 and 51380).

Although the Port of Bristol Authority (PBA) had closed down their rail operation in 1983, BR then undertook to work any remaining traffic over PBA lines using BR locos and crew. On 5 October 1983 special train 6Z35 has arrived from Ince and Elton behind No. 47258, and is seen at Hallen Marsh. The train was a trial load of fertiliser. To work forward into the PBA Chittening Estate a Class 08 No. 08949 was specially provided, there being no regular shunting loco at Hallen Marsh at that time.

There were several freight customers in the Avonmouth area providing significant traffic. One of these was the Fisons tank farm adjacent to St Andrews Road station, which dispatched trains to other Fisons locations at Immingham, Ipswich and Plymouth. Immingham-allocated No. 31238 is seen passing Hallen Marsh with 7Z67, a special from Ipswich to Avonmouth Fisons formed of discharged ammonium nitrate tanks, on 5 October 1983.

Old Oak Common-allocated No. 31296 is on local freight trip duty at Avonmouth on 11 February 1980 and is seen just north of Smoke Lane crossing with three VDAs. This short stretch of double track connected the BR network at Hallen Marsh to the extensive internal rail network that served the Commonwealth Smelting Works.

The Commonwealth Smelting Company had a pair of Sentinel four-wheel diesel-hydraulic locos to shunt the rail network at the smelting works at Hallen Marsh. The principle traffic was coke which was received each weekday from South Wales. One of the Sentinels is seen surrounded by HTVs of coke as BR supervisor Jack Hyde talks to the loco crew on 26 January 1982.

Bristol-allocated Class 121 Pressed Steel single power cars worked many of the services on the Severn Beach line. On 5 February 1981 set B132 (vehicle No. 55032) approaches St Andrews Road with the 09.05 Severn Beach to Bristol Temple Meads service. The grassy area to the left is PBA property and is the site of the former Avonmouth Royal Edward Yard, which closed in 1977. On the right is a temporary tip siding; this later became the site of the reception sidings for the Bristol Bulk Handling Terminal.

On weekdays there were fifteen passenger workings each way on the Severn Beach Line, and on 5 February 1981 single power car B132 (No. 55032) is seen again approaching St Andrews Road, this time on a service to Severn Beach. In the background is Avonmouth Town Goods Yard signal box, which was one of five mechanical boxes still open in the Avonmouth area at the time. The siding on the left leads into Fisons tank farm.

Filton Bank in north Bristol had been a stretch of four-track main line, but in 1984 the tracks were reduced from four to two. On 30 September 1981 Tinsley-allocated No. 45007 is running on the Down Filton main line as it approaches Stapleton Road with a cross-country service for the West Country. These two lines were the ones taken out of use and removed in 1984.

The Up and Down Filton relief lines were retained through Stapleton Road and Lawrence Hill stations following the 1984 rationalisation. Eastleigh-allocated No. 33024 powers through Stapleton Road on the Up Filton relief line with a service from Portsmouth Harbour to Cardiff Central on 30 September 1981.

Lawrence Hill station only had platforms on the relief lines, the platforms serving the main lines having been taken out of use in the 1970s. A special parcels working comprising one GUV and one CCT passes Lawrence Hill behind No. 31312, heading towards Bristol on the Down Filton main line on 2 June 1981.

The yard at Lawrence Hill was still busy in the early 1980s; Aberthaw Cement and Ketton Cement both had terminals in the yard and the yard pilot also worked trips down the Avonside branch. On 28 September 1983, yard pilot No. 08949 is seen detaching traffic from 6B46, the 06.30 Severn Tunnel Junction to Bridgwater Speedlink service.

Southern Region Class 33 locos took over services on the Portsmouth Harbour to Bristol and Cardiff route in 1980 as well as some services between Bristol and Weymouth. Eastleigh-allocated locos were normally rostered for the duties, but on 20 September 1983 Hither Green's No. 33065 is seen passing Kingsland Road in Bristol while working the 09.10 Portsmouth Harbour to Cardiff Central service.

The Portsmouth to Cardiff route eventually received an hourly service during the day, but in the early years some services did not operate over the whole route. Departing Bristol Temple Meads on 25 April 1983 is No. 33027 *Earl Mountbatten of Burma* with 2C26, the 10.25 Bristol Temple Meads to Cardiff Central.

Class 40s were infrequent visitors to the Bristol area in the 1980s, but on Saturday 1 September 1984 a special relief train brought one member of the class into Bristol. The 10.10 Edinburgh to Birmingham New Street had been extended to Bristol Temple Meads and was hauled by No. 40122. Formerly numbered D200, No. 40122 had been overhauled and reinstated into traffic earlier in the year, outshopped in Brunswick Green. The empty stock is seen departing Bristol and heading back north.

In 1982 Bristol had an allocation of sixteen Class 117 Pressed Steel suburban three-car sets. These worked services to Cardiff, Gloucester, Weymouth, Weston-super-Mare, Taunton and Severn Beach. On 15 June 1982 two sets are seen at Bristol Temple Meads Platforms 12 and 11. Nearest the camera is set B437, formed of vehicle Nos 51338, 59504 and 51380.

Three trains stand in front of the 1878-built train shed at Bristol Temple Meads on 9 June 1983. In Platforms 3 and 4 is the 07.05 HST service from Plymouth to York. On the Up through line is Stratford-allocated No. 31125 at the head of the 3B20 Paddington to Bristol parcels. On Platform 6 is a service for Taunton formed by Class 117 Pressed Steel set B436, comprising vehicles Nos 51334, 59500 and 51376.

On 5 August 1983 a trainload of new vans has arrived from Dover and is being shunted to Pylle Hill yard for unloading by the Bristol Temple Meads station pilot, No. 08756. The vans will then be taken by road to Royal Portbury Dock. Above the loco, and covered in scaffolding, is the Bristol & Exeter Building, which housed the headquarters offices of the West of England Division. The building was originally the headquarters of the Bristol & Exeter Railway.

Although the Royal Portbury Dock had opened in 1978 it was not originally rail connected, and it was not until the summer of 1983 that BR gained any traffic to or from the port. Trainloads of new vehicles were loaded and unloaded at both Temple Meads station and Pylle Hill yard, with road haulage to and from Portbury. Bristol Temple Meads pilot No. 08951 shunts a train of cartics that had been loaded with imported cars in the motorail dock on 5 July 1983.

Laira-allocated No. 50047 *Swiftsure* stands at Platform 12 at Bristol Temple Meads on 5 July 1983 with a train for the west as GPO staff unload mail. In the background is Bristol Temple Meads Loco signal box. Although it had closed as a signal box it was still known as 'Shed Box', and from here staff controlled the movement of locos to and from Bath Road depot.

A view of the stabling sidings at Bristol Bath Road depot on 17 May 1982. The locos on view include three Bath Road-allocated locos, Nos 31419, 31231 and 31401, and visiting loco Nos 31326 from Toton, 25160 from Crewe Diesel and 47166 from Cardiff Canton. The DMU is standing outside the Heavy Lift Shop, though normally the Bristol-allocated DMUs were fuelled and maintained at Marsh Junction.

In 1983 the Daily Shed at Bath Road was rebuilt and extended in length to accommodate three-car DMUs to enable the Bristol DMU fleet to be fuelled and maintained at Bath Road. On 13 August 1983 Hither Green-allocated No. 33055 and Landore-allocated No. 47575 stand outside the newly extended shed.

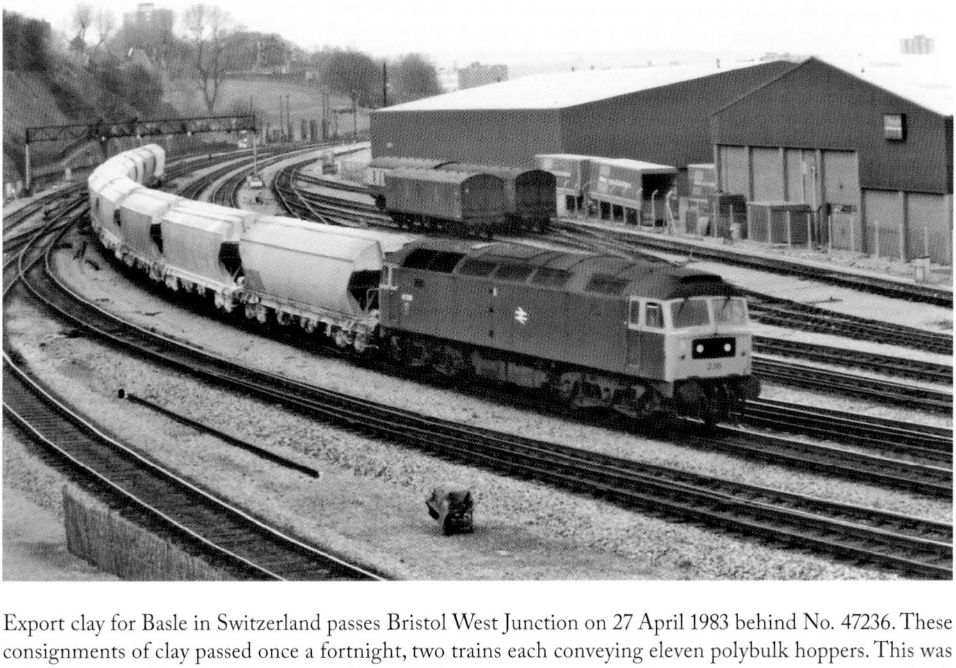

Export clay for Basle in Switzerland passes Bristol West Junction on 27 April 1983 behind No. 47236. These consignments of clay passed once a fortnight, two trains each conveying eleven polybulk hoppers. This was 6Z94, the 07.45 Tavistock Junction to Dover. When returning empty, the twenty-two wagons came back combined as a single train.

To the west of Bristol Temple Meads there were four running lines, the Up and Down mains, the Up relief, and the engine and carriage line. The engine and carriage line was used by empty stock movements to and from Malago Vale carriage sidings, seen here on 27 April 1983 as No. 33027 *Earl Moutnbatten of Burma* approaches Bristol West Junction with 5O75, empty stock for the 12.14 Bristol Temple Meads to Portsmouth Harbour service.

Most empty stock movements between Bristol Temple Meads and Malago Vale carriage sidings were booked to pass through the carriage washing machine, which was located on a loop off the engine and carriage line. The carriage washing machine is seen from Victoria Park on 11 February 1980 as Toton-allocated No. 45051 passes through. This loco was one of the last of the class to retain headcode boxes.

In 1980 there had been only seven through services on weekdays from Portsmouth Harbour to Bristol, with some being extended to Cardiff, but by 1986 this had increased to thirteen a day. On 16 June 1986 Hither Green-allocated No. 33060 approaches Bath Spa with the 15.10 Portsmouth Harbour to Cardiff Central.

Bradford-on-Avon was served by all trains on the Bristol to Weymouth route but not by all services on the Portsmouth to Bristol route, some of which ran fast from Salisbury to Bath Spa. The 16.10 Portsmouth Harbour to Cardiff Central is seen running non-stop through Bradford-on-Avon behind Hither Green's No. 33051 on 20 August 1983.

At Trowbridge Eastleigh-allocated No. 33002 arrives with the 15.10 Portsmouth Harbour to Bristol Temple Meads service on 20 August 1983. The station building on the left, which dated from 1847/8, was demolished in 1984. The footbridge was dismantled in 1989 but has now been restored and erected at Williton on the West Somerset Railway.

The 14.10 Portsmouth Harbour to Bristol Temple Meads service passes Hawkeridge Junction just north of Westbury behind another Hither Green-allocated Class 33, No. 33062, on 16 June 1986. The lines on the left curve around to Heywood Road Junction and provide a diversionary route for trains from Bristol towards London.

Westbury North Junction on 3 January 1981 as the 07.14 Penzance to Paddington service departs Westbury. A set of empty ARC-liveried PGA hoppers are standing on the Patney Siding. To the right of the fence is the site for the future Westbury Panel Signal Box.

A returning midweek ballast drop passes Westbury Panel signal box, which is under construction, on 23 August 1983. Class 31s were regularly used on these services, and Toton-allocated No. 31171 had departed Bristol East Depot at 07.15 and run via Westbury to Woodborough and back. The formation of ten dogfish hoppers and a shark plough van was a common one at the time. The permanent way gang are riding on the platform of the third hopper.

Westbury Panel signal box opened in May 1984 when four mechanical boxes at Heywood Road Junction, Fairwood Junction, Hawkeridge and Westbury closed. On 17 July 1985 one of the Bath Road pool of Class 56 locos, No. 56048, stands outside the signal box. At that date Class 56s worked the majority of the Mendip stone trains. From 1986 American-built Class 59s owned by Foster Yeoman, and also later by ARC, would take over much of the work.

Bristol East Depot downside yard was the most important civil engineers yard in the west of England. In addition to weekend engineering trains, many midweek ballast drops would start from there. Having run round its train of a shark plough van and ten empty dogfish ballast hoppers from Woodborough, No. 31171 departs Westbury on the return journey to Bristol East Depot on 23 August 1983. Westbury signal box would close in May 1984 when the new panel signal box opened.

In 1986 the majority of services from the West Country to Paddington were worked by HSTs, though there were still some loco-hauled services. The 10.00 Penzance to Paddington service departs Westbury behind Laira-allocated No. 50014 *Warspite* on 16 June 1986.

To supplement the Portsmouth Harbour and Weymouth services there was a number of peak hour local services worked by DMUs to and from Bristol. The 17.40 service from Bristol Temple terminates at Westbury on 21 June 1984 formed by Class 101 Metro-Cammell set C823, comprising vehicles Nos 51505, 59082 and 51511.

By 1983 the refurbishment of the Class 50 fleet was well underway. No. 50011 *Centurion* was one of the later locos to be dealt with, and was released from Doncaster Works in May of that year. It is seen here on a summer Saturday service at Westbury while working the 11.14 Paignton to Paddington on 20 August 1983.

In 1983 there were eight services each way between Westbury and Weymouth on weekdays, four of these extending to or from Bristol. On summer Saturdays there were nine trains each way, some running through to Cardiff. On Saturday 20 August 1983, Gloucester-built Class 119 cross-country set B586, formed of vehicles Nos 51077, 59420 and 51105, is seen at Westbury when about to work the 14.57 service to Weymouth.

Although Bristol to Weymouth is 87 miles, and the journey could take over two and a half hours, most services were worked by Bristol-based DMUs of various types. Either cross-country or suburban DMU sets could be allocated to the route. On Saturday 20 August 1983 Pressed Steel suburban Class 117 set B434, formed of vehicles Nos 51372, 59490 and 51414, waits at Westbury to work the 13.00 service to Weymouth.

The re-signalling of the Westbury area in 1984 brought with it a simplified track layout and, as a result, the number of platforms were reduced from four to three. The former Platform 1 (the Down Salisbury line) was taken out of use and became the Down reception line for the yard. Standing at the new Platform 1 on 17 July 1985 is the 15.10 Bristol Temple Meads to Portsmouth Harbour service behind Eastleigh-allocated No. 33023.

In 1983 the loco allocation at Bristol Bath Road included eighteen Class 37s, all of which were air-braked examples. They were often employed in pairs on stone traffic, from ARC Tytherington quarry and the two large Mendip quarries, ARC Whatley and the Foster Yeoman quarry at Merehead. On 23 August 1983 Nos 37176 and 37159 are seen at Westbury.

At weekends, with the weekly stone train programme completed, many locos would return to Westbury depot. On Saturday 20 August 1983 Class 37s and Class 47s are seen stabled in the depot. Up yard pilot No. 08900 is shunting civil engineer's wagons to form a train ready for weekend engineering work.

In addition to the Mendip stone traffic there were also two bitumen terminals in the area, at Frome and Cranmore. On 21 June 1984 No. 47279 is on a Westbury area local freight trip working with loaded bitumen tanks for Cranmore, and is seen having come to a stand at Witham.

Stage 3 of the Westbury re-signalling scheme took effect in November 1984 when Witham signal box closed. On 21 June 1984 preliminary work is already underway at Witham as the 11.05 Weymouth to Westbury service passes. Class 117 Pressed Steel DMU set B437 is formed of vehicle Nos 51338, 59504 and 51380.

The 14.30 Weston-super-Mare to Paddington service formed by HST set No. 253037 passes through the site of Flax Bourton station on 6 November 1986. This was the second station at Flax Bourton; it opened in 1893 and closed to passengers in December 1963. The first station, which dated from 1860, had been located further into the cutting towards Bristol.

Approaching Flax Bourton on 6 November 1986 behind No. 50041 *Bulwark* is a long-distance cross-country service 1S71, the 07.30 Penzance to Aberdeen, which was not scheduled to reach the Granite City until 21.57. The sidings on the right served a Ministry of Fuel and Power underground fuel depot, but had been out of use for many years by this date.

Once Southern Region Class 33 locos had taken over operation of the Portsmouth Harbour to Bristol and Cardiff services, the loco diagrams also included some local services from Bristol to Weston-super-Mare and Taunton. On 25 June 1983 Hither Green-allocated No. 33048 runs into Nailsea & Backwell with the 15.10 Portsmouth Harbour to Weston-super-Mare.

Nailsea & Backwell station was opened by the Bristol & Exeter Railway in 1841. The station is served by local services from Bristol to Weston-super-Mare and Taunton, as well as some services to and from Paddington. On 25 June 1983 Class 119 Gloucester-built set B577 calls, formed of vehicle Nos 51063, 59422 and 51091. The service is the 15.45 Taunton to Bristol Temple Meads.

Any class of DMU allocated to Bristol could be seen on local services to Weston-super-Mare and Taunton. Class 117 Pressed Steel set B437, formed of vehicle Nos 51338, 59504 and 51380, is working the 16.33 Bristol Temple Meads to Taunton service at Nailsea & Backwell on 25 June 1983.

The Bristol & Exeter route runs virtually dead straight across the North Somerset Levels for almost 9 miles from just west of Nailsea & Backwell station to near Worle Junction. Shortly after departure from Nailsea & Backwell is Gateshead-allocated No. 47566 at Chelvey with the 15.25 Bristol Temple Meads to Weston-super-Mare on 6 November 1986.

Since their introduction HSTs had worked services from Paddington to Weston-super-Mare, and on summer Saturdays there were hourly services during the day. On Saturday 25 June 1983 the 13.35 Paddington to Weston-super-Mare service, formed by set 253016, is seen approaching Yatton.

Bath Road-allocated No. 47148 speeds through Yatton with the summer Saturday 13.06 Birmingham New Street to Paignton service on 25 June 1983. Yatton was formerly the junction for branches to Clevedon and the Cheddar Valley line. The former Cheddar Valley bay platform is on the right, the branch having closed in 1963.

The straight and level nature of the route in North Somerset can be seen in this view on 25 June 1983. Cardiff Canton-allocated No. 47072 has just passed the Yatton goods loops and approaches the station with the 13.00 Paignton to Swansea service.

The Bristol & Exeter Railway first reached Weston-super-Mare in 1841 via a single track branch line, which was originally worked by horses. In this view the gasworks sidings to the right follow the alignment of the original route, which was crossed by the later loop line in 1884. The 16.15 from Bristol Temple Meads arrives at Weston-super-Mare behind No. 50035 *Ark Royal* on 30 April 1983.

The current station dates from 1884 and was formerly known as Weston-super-Mare General. It replaced the 1866 station, which was located off to the right of this view. The 1866 station then became the goods depot, but that closed in the 1960s. On 11 January 1982 an unidentified Class 47 loco stands at Weston-super-Mare with a cross-country service for the north.

On 30 April 1983 two DMUs are seen working afternoon commuter services at Weston-super-Mare. Class 117 Pressed Steel set B426, formed of vehicles Nos 51364, 59516 and 51406, is about to work the 17.22 departure for Bristol Temple Meads. Class 101 Metro-Cammell set C823, formed of vehicles Nos 51505, 59082 and 51511, has just arrived on the 16.45 service from Bristol Temple Meads.

A couple of loco-hauled services started or terminated at Weston-super-Mare each day. The station shunter is just about to uncouple Eastleigh-allocated No. 33003, which has arrived with the 15.10 service from Portsmouth Harbour to Weston-super-Mare on 23 July 1983.

On 24 August 1981 the 13.21 Liverpool Lime Street to Plymouth service was heavily delayed and a Control Special train had been run in the same timings from Bristol to Taunton. The 17.09 Bristol Temple Meads to Taunton special is seen departing Weston-super-Mare behind Bath Road-allocated No. 31421. It is passing Gloucester-built Class 119 DMU set C571, formed of vehicle Nos 51052, 59282 and 51080.

By 1982 traditional vacuum-braked freight trains were becoming rarer on the West of England Division. Seen behind an unidentified Class 47 loco at Bleadon & Uphill is 6B46, the 06.30 Severn Tunnel Junction to Bridgwater vacuum-braked freight service, on 15 June 1982. It is passing beneath Devil's Bridge, a brick arch which was designed by Isambard Kingdom Brunel. It is one of the highest spans on the route.

HSTs were introduced onto cross-country services in the early 1980s. By 1982 eight of the weekday cross-country services from Plymouth were worked by HSTs, with three services still being worked by locos and coaches. On 15 June 1982 1E61, the 07.55 Plymouth to Leeds HST, approaches the site of Bleadon & Uphill station.

On summer Saturdays, 3C20, the 05.20 Paddington to Plymouth parcels, was scheduled to recess at Bristol Temple Meads until 17.10 in the afternoon. It is seen here approaching Highbridge behind Bath Road-allocated No. 47283 at 17.27 on 28 July 1984. The facing crossover gives access to Highbridge (Up reversible) goods loop.

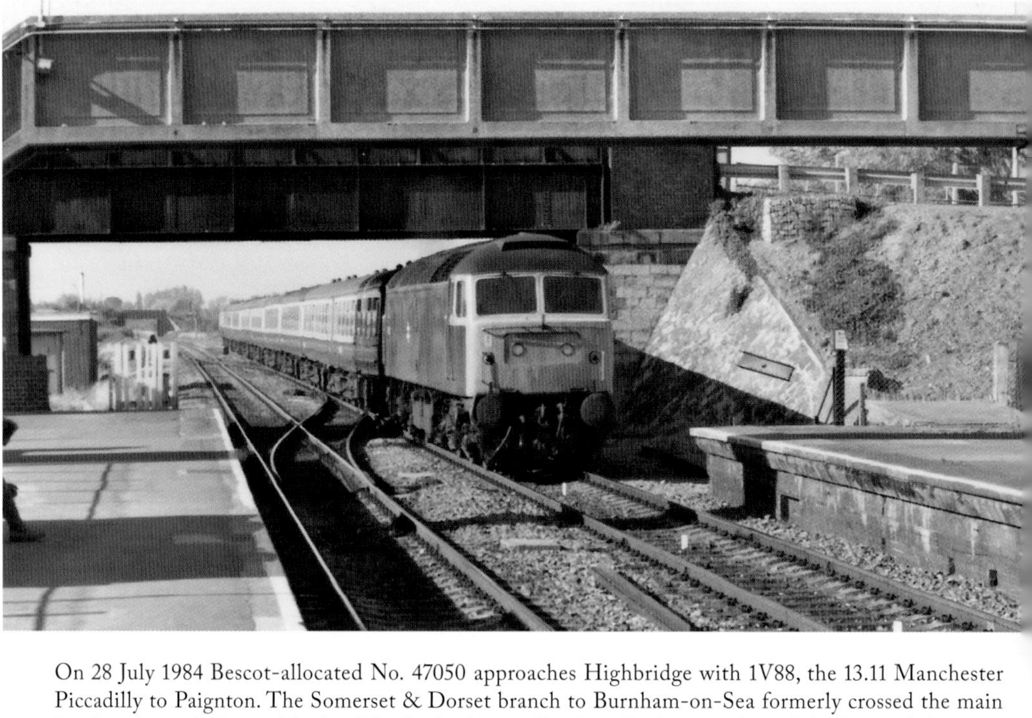

On 28 July 1984 Bescot-allocated No. 47050 approaches Highbridge with 1V88, the 13.11 Manchester Piccadilly to Paignton. The Somerset & Dorset branch to Burnham-on-Sea formerly crossed the main line here beneath the road bridge. The footbridge is a Southern Railway product of the Exmouth Junction concrete works and at one time also linked to the adjacent S&D station.

Toton-allocated No. 45124 rushes through Highbridge with 1V86, the 13.44 Birmingham New Street to Paignton on Saturday 28 July 1984.

On Saturday 1 September 1984 a cross-country HST set working 1V66, the 06.28 Bradford Exchange to Paignton, approaches Bridgwater at speed. It is passing the UKF depot, which received regular trainloads of fertiliser from Ince & Elton.

At the start of the 1980s Bridgwater Yard was shunted each weekday by a Class 08 loco which arrived working 8B05, the 07.00 Taunton to Bridgwater freight trip. On 12 September 1980 No. 08281 has commenced work in Bridgwater Yard. The discharged nuclear flask wagons had arrived on the train and are about to be positioned under the gantry crane.

By 1983 the nuclear flask traffic to and from Sellafield no longer passed on the ordinary wagonload network, but was conveyed on special dedicated services. Toton-allocated No. 47202 arrives at Bridgwater on 9 August 1983 with 7V52, the 17.22 MWO Sellafield to Bridgwater. The loaded flasks would return back north later that day on 7M53.

On 12 September 1980 Bath Road-allocated No. 47246 calls at Bridgwater with 1E30, the 08.15 Plymouth to Leeds. When HSTs were introduced onto the cross-country network the service was accelerated, though this also meant some station stops were subsequently omitted, and places like Bridgwater lost out.

At 10.58 on Saturday 1 September 1984, and running on time, Laira-allocated No. 50043 *Eagle* speeds through Bridgwater with 1M08, the 09.24 Paignton to Birmingham New Street service.

One of the Bath Road-allocated ETH-fitted Class 31/4s, No. 31422 is seen shunting at Bridgwater on Friday 1 May 1981. It had been provided as an additional loco that day to carry out shunts to form up trains ready for weekend engineering work. The grampus wagons are loaded with blanketing sand.

Bridgwater station was opened in 1841 and the original Bristol & Exeter Railway buildings still remain. On Saturday 1 September 1984 another Bath Road-allocated Class 31, this time No. 31286, calls with 2C04, the 06.50 Bristol Temple Meads to Taunton local service.

Most summer Saturday trains to the West Country did not call at Bridgwater, but one that did was 1V64, the 07.17 Derby to Penzance. It is seen on time standing at Bridgwater on Saturday 1 September 1984 behind No. 45040 *The King's Shropshire Light Infantry*. The loco was one of a number with an isolated steam heating boiler. These were normally confined to freight work, but were pressed into passenger work on summer Saturdays.

In 1931 Cogload Junction had been remodelled to a flying junction and four tracks were provided from there to Taunton. On 25 May 1985 Laira-allocated No. 50016 *Barham* is running on the Down relief line with 3C20, the 05.20 Paddington to Plymouth parcels. In March 1986 the two (outer) relief lines were taken out of use, and in April 1986 Cogload signal box closed as part of the Exeter re-signalling scheme.

The ETH-fitted Class 45/1 fleet was allocated to Toton and mainly worked services on the Midland Main Line to St Pancras, but summer Saturdays brought many of them to the West Country. On Saturday 25 May 1985 eight members of the class had passed through Taunton. In the late afternoon No. 45129 heads the 15.18 Birmingham New Street to Paignton service near Cogload.

On Saturday 25 May 1985 Laira-allocated No. 50009 *Conqueror* is approaching Cogload on the Up relief line with 1E32, the 16.43 Paignton to Leeds cross-country service. This was one of fifteen different members of the class to pass in eight hours.

Not all passenger services were booked to call at Taunton, particularly on summer Saturdays; usually the through trains were booked to pass on the main lines. One train booked to run non-stop through Taunton was 1C33, the 10.45 Paddington to Penzance. It is seen approaching Taunton on the Down main with power car No. 43170 leading on 1 September 1984.

Accelerating away from the Taunton station stop is Toton-allocated No. 45002 working 1M22, the 11.28 Paignton to Manchester Piccadilly, on 1 September 1984. Part of Taunton East Yard can be seen, as well as the Taunton Goods avoiding lines and Taunton East Junction signal box, and to the right is part of Taunton concrete works.

The view looking east from the platform at Taunton on 23 July 1983 as a Scottish visitor, No. 47102 from Eastfield depot, approaches on the Down main line. The wagons on the left are loaded with concrete beams manufactured in Taunton concrete works, while on the right the air-braked open wagons are standing in the East Yard.

Taunton was as far west as the Bristol-based DMU fleet normally worked. On 1 September 1984 Class 118 BRCW set B473, formed of vehicles Nos 51316, 59483 and 51331, arrives on 2C36, the 13.55 Bristol Temple Meads to Taunton service. It then returned to Bristol at 15.17.

Toton-allocated No. 45136 is departing from the Down platform at Taunton on Saturday 1 September 1984 with 1V67, the 07.59 Nottingham to Paignton. On summer Saturdays standby locos were provided at various locations, including Taunton. No. 47318 is stabled in the background. The middle island platform in the foreground serving the Up and Down main lines had been taken out of use in 1967 and had no passenger facilities.

Taunton continued to be a loco stabling point and traincrew signing-on point long after the steam shed had closed and been demolished in the 1960s. Class 08s for shunting and the local trip work to Bridgwater had been supplied by Bristol Bath Road, but later Laira-allocated locos were diagrammed to shunt at Taunton. On 12 March 1988 Laira's No. 08576 is seen stabled adjacent to the workshop building.

When the Class 50 fleet was transferred to the Western Region in the 1970s they were shared between Bath Road, Laira and Old Oak Common depots, but by 1982 all were based at either Laira or Old Oak. On 1 September 1984 No. 50003 *Temeraire,* one of the Laira-based locos, is signalled onto the Up relief platform line at Taunton with 1A59, the 12.56 Paignton to Paddington service.

Bath Road depot maintained a large allocation of Class 47s. One of these, No. 47250, is seen from Forty Steps Bridge at Taunton West as it departs from the station on 24 August 1981. The semaphore signals here were replaced by multiple aspect signals in May 1986 in Stage 4B of the Exeter re-signalling scheme when Taunton West Station signal box closed.

The additional trains that ran on summer Saturdays brought many Class 45s to the West Country. On Saturday 28 July 1984 No. 45006 *Honourable Artillery Company* was one of fifteen members of the class to pass through Taunton. It is seen at Taunton West with 1E64, the 10.35 Penzance to Leeds.

Speeding past Taunton Fairwater Yard on Saturday 23 July 1983 is a HST set forming the 13.45 Paddington to Penzance service. This train ran non-stop between Reading and Exeter St Davids. In the background is Fairwater PAD (Pre-Assembly Depot), which had opened in 1960. The PAD built up new track sections ready for relaying work, and was the usual home for shunting loco PWM 652, which can be seen in the yard.

West of Taunton the railway crossed the busy Silk Mills Road, and significant queues of traffic could build up at Silk Mill Crossing, particularly on summer Saturdays. On 23 July 1983 Toton-allocated No. 45072 approaches the crossing with 1V64, the 07.41 Derby to Penzance.

Crewe Diesel Depot's non-boilered No. 47340 was one of many freight locos to be pressed into passenger use on summer Saturdays. It is seen passing the site of Norton Fitzwarren station with 1V73, the 08.20 Liverpool Lime Street to Paignton on 23 July 1983. The Taunton Cider Company had taken over part of the old station site and became an important freight customer, dispatching cider in vans via the Speedlink network.

Oak Common-allocated No. 47500 *Great Western* passes beneath the footbridge of the former Norton Fitzwarren station with a train from the west on 23 July 1983. The loco was always kept looking smart and the next day would be on Royal Train duty. Norton Fitzwarren station had closed in October 1961, and the building in the background was the former railway hotel.

To add variety to the procession of summer Saturday passenger trains is 1E21, the 14.15 Plymouth to Leeds parcels, seen passing through the site of Wellington station on 25 May 1985 behind Toton-allocated No. 45029. Wellington signal box closed in March 1986 as part of the Exeter re-signalling scheme.

On 17 August 1985 Laira-allocated No. 50008 *Thunderer* races down Wellington Bank at Beambridge. At its steepest point the bank is 1 in 80. It was when descending Wellington Bank on 9 May 1904 that *City of Truro* was recorded as traveling at 100 mph.

The summit of the line between Taunton and Exeter is just west of Whiteball Tunnel. A Down loop was provided to enable freight trains that had just completed the climb to be recessed. On 25 May 1985 Laira-allocated No. 50019 *Ramillies* passes the loop with a train for the west.

The climb up to Whiteball from the Exeter direction is not so severe, being no steeper than 1 in 115. On 25 May 1985 one of Old Oak Common's named Class 47s, No. 47513 *Severn*, nears the summit at Whiteball with a train from the west. The signal box at Whiteball was closed in March 1986.

At Tiverton Junction, Old Oak Common-allocated No. 50039 *Implacable* passes non-stop with the 09.40 Paddington to Penzance on 25 May 1985. On the right the short section of track is the remains of the Hemyock Branch, which had closed in 1975, having latterly only carried milk traffic.

On the Down main at Tiverton Junction is Tinsley-allocated No. 45026 with a heavily delayed 1V58, the 22.20 Glasgow Central to Paignton service on 28 July 1984. To the left is the Esso oil terminal, which had received block trains from the refinery at Fawley. The terminal had closed in 1983.

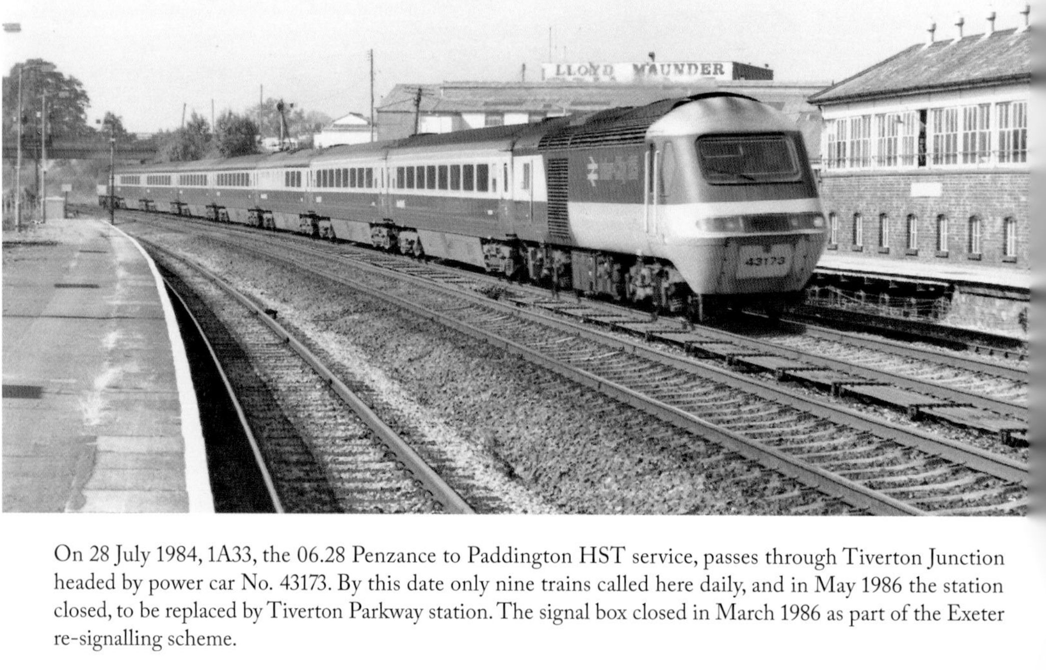

On 28 July 1984, 1A33, the 06.28 Penzance to Paddington HST service, passes through Tiverton Junction headed by power car No. 43173. By this date only nine trains called here daily, and in May 1986 the station closed, to be replaced by Tiverton Parkway station. The signal box closed in March 1986 as part of the Exeter re-signalling scheme.

In the West of England Division there were Motorail terminals at Bristol Temple Meads, Newton Abbot and St Austell. Passing through Tiverton Junction on 28 July 1984 is 1C14, the 07.30 Paddington to St Austell Motorail, behind Cardiff Canton-allocated No. 47061.

A Paddington-bound HST is about to pass non-stop through Tiverton Junction on the Up main line on 24 August 1981. The loops here were retained after the station closed in 1986, though the freight loops at Wellington, Whiteball, and Hele & Bradninch were all removed as part of the Exeter Area re-signalling scheme.

On summer Saturdays there was a steady stream of trains heading to and from the West Country for several hours during the middle of the day. On 25 May 1985 one of ten trains to pass within the hour was the 09.55 Penzance to Leeds, seen just south of Tiverton Junction behind Cardiff Canton-allocated No. 47597.

Passing Cowley Bridge Junction on 21 April 1982 is Laira-allocated No. 50050 *Fearless* with 1V90, the 13.20 Liverpool Lime Street to Plymouth. This junction has had repeated problems over the years as a result of flooding from the Rivers Exe and Creedy. A culvert had been built under the line at this point to relieve the flood water. Despite this the fresh ballast seen on the Barnstaple line is evidence of recent repair work.

On 11 July 1984 a Plymouth-based BRCW-built Class 118 DMU set passes over Cowley Bridge Junction. Set P466, formed of vehicles Nos 51308, 59475 and 51323, is working 2B77, the 15.06 Barnstaple to Exeter St Davids. This section of the Barnstaple route had been singled in 1965 when the bridges spanning the River Exe, seen in the background, were renewed.

Waiting to depart from Exeter Riverside Yard on 11 July 1984 is an engineers' train headed by Toton-allocated No. 45049 *The Staffordshire Regiment, The Prince of Wales's.* The turbot wagons loaded with ballast have come from Meldon Quarry, and the train has been into Riverside Yard to reverse.

The output of track ballast from Meldon Quarry was considerable: up to six trains ran on weekdays, and two of these were for the Southern Region. On 31 October 1983 Laira-allocated No. 50009 *Conqueror* approaches Crediton with twenty-one empty sealion and seacow hoppers for Meldon.

The Exeter & Crediton Railway had a complicated history. It was involved in the 'Battle of the Gauges' and was at one time laid as broad gauge, but eventually became part of the London & South Western Railway. On 31 October 1983 the 10.10 Barnstaple to Exeter St Davids departs from Crediton. BRCW-built Class 118 set P462 is formed of vehicles Nos 51304, 59477 and 51319.

The Barnstaple passenger service generally consisted of nine or ten trains each way on weekdays. Two services each way were booked for locos and coaches, but the majority of the services were worked by DMUs. On 31 October 1983 another Plymouth-based Class 118 set is seen at Barnstaple. Set P463, formed of vehicles Nos 51305, 59472 and 51320, waits to work the 14.28 service to Exmouth.

A view of the west end of Meldon Quarry on 9 July 1981 with the resident quarry pilot loco, Laira-allocated No. 08668, at work. The hard hornfels rock was considered to be the best ballast available by the Western and Southern Regions, and up to six trains a day could be loaded. A typical day's departures would be: 06.49 to Exeter Riverside, 09.05 to Exeter Riverside, 11.33 to Salisbury, 14.46 to Bristol East Depot, 19.34 to Salisbury and 22.35 to Exeter Riverside.

A busy scene at Exeter St Davids at 08.22 on 7 November 1983. Eastleigh-allocated No. 33016 is arriving with the 07.13 service from Barnstaple. On the left, No. 47094 waits to shunt the empty GUV from the rear of the Barnstaple stock onto the empty news van train for Old Oak Common. In the loco spur is Toton-allocated No. 45059 *Royal Engineer*. Exeter Middle signal box closed on 29 March 1985 as part of Stage 1A of the Exeter re-signalling scheme.

By July 1984 preliminary work for the Exeter re-signalling scheme was underway at Exeter St Davids, with new signals installed but not yet in use. The summer Saturday train service is in full swing as Tinsley-allocated No. 45015 rolls into Exeter St Davids with 1V67, the 07.59 Nottingham to Paignton on 28 July 1984. As before, the crossing keeper keeps a close watch on proceedings.

On 29 March 1985 the new Exeter panel signal box opened, and on the same date Exeter Middle signal box closed. The new revised track layout at the north end of Exeter St Davids is seen on 9 July 1985. The 06.50 Swindon to Penzance service runs into Platform 1 behind Toton-allocated No. 45124 as March-allocated No. 31164 heads north, running light diesel.

In 1985 Laira had received an allocation of thirteen newly built Class 142 railbus sets known as 'skippers', but these proved unsuccessful on the steep and curving routes of the West Country. In 1987 a number of Class 108 Derby Lightweight DMUs were transferred to the WR as a replacement. This was the first time Class 108 DMUs had been allocated to the WR, and Laira received some of the sets. On 12 March 1988 a Class 108 set stands in Platform 2 at Exeter St Davids. Set P955, formed of vehicles Nos 51933 and 52054, had previously been based at Newton Heath.

On Saturday 28 July 1984 Cardiff Canton-allocated No. 47603 is seen at Exeter St Davids, hauling a failed HST set. The train is 1V61, the 06.50 Birmingham New Street to Paignton, which is running ninety minutes late. Later that afternoon No. 47603 hauled the HST set back north.

One of the results of the Exeter re-signalling was the removal of the Down main line between Platforms 1 and 3, and the loss of this line caused problems for freight trains to find pathways up to Exeter Central and Exmouth Junction. On 17 July 1985 a pair of Class 50s are awaiting departure. On the left at Platform 3, Laira's No. 50014 *Warspite* is working the 08.11 departure to Waterloo. At Platform 1, No. 50047 *Swiftsure,* also of Laira depot, calls with the 06.35 Bristol Temple Meads to Plymouth service. This train was booked here for eight minutes to unload parcels.

There was no carriage maintenance facility at Exeter so empty stock off the Waterloo to Exeter route was sent to Newton Abbot each evening. On 16 July 1980 Bath Road-allocated No. 31118 departs from Exeter St Davids to Newton Abbot. When the depot at Newton Abbot closed in 1981, empty stock was then sent to Laira depot for maintenance.

The Waterloo to Exeter route had been dieselised in 1964, initially by WR Warship diesel-hydraulics. Southern Region Class 33s took over the work in October 1971, and Eastleigh-based locos were diagrammed to the duties until May 1980. An additional service that ran during the summer of 1984 was 1V08, the 10.00 Waterloo to Exeter St Davids. It is seen arriving at Exeter on 28 July 1984 behind Hither Green's No. 33039.

The complex layout at Exeter West is seen as Toton's No. 45051 arrives at Exeter St Davids with 1M86, the 10.00 Paignton to Liverpool Lime Street, on 28 July 1984. Exeter West signal box had a frame containing 131 levers. The box had been built in 1913 and would close in May 1985 when the new Exeter panel signal box replaced it. Standing beneath the box is No. 50030 *Repulse,* which was one of Old Oak Common's Class 50 fleet.

The first Class 25 locos were allocated to Laira in 1971 to replace the remaining Class 22 diesel-hydraulics, the last of which were withdrawn in October that year. Laira retained an allocation of around ten Class 25s until November 1980, when the last two members of the class were transferred away. There were normally three or four at work in the Exeter area on local freight and passenger services, particularly to Barnstaple and North Devon. On 8 April 1980 No. 25155 stands at the stabling point at Exeter St Davids. In October of that year it would be re-allocated north to Wigan Springs Branch.

Exeter panel signal box opened on 29 March 1985 when the mechanical signal boxes at Cowley Bridge Junction and Exeter Middle both closed. The area controlled by the new box expanded until by October 1987 the route controlled stretched from Totnes in the west to Durston and Athelney, both to the east of Cogload Junction. The new signal box is seen under construction on 9 July 1983.

The former GWR steam shed at Exeter St Davids lost its last allocation of locomotives in 1963 and although the roof was removed, it remained in use as a stabling point. A small single-road shed was constructed in 1980 within the walls of the former four-track shed. On 28 July 1984 five locos are stabled in and around the old shed, including Nos 50006 *Neptune*, 31273 and 47187.

From May 1980, Western Region Class 50s replaced the Southern Region Class 33s working the Waterloo to Exeter route. On 11 March 1983 Laira-allocated No. 50003 *Temeraire* is seen at Exeter Central with 1O10, the 09.38 Exeter St Davids to Waterloo. The former goods yard was in use as a Blue Circle Cement depot and received block trains from Westbury cement works. At this date Premier Transport also used the siding on the extreme right to unload Guinness traffic from Park Royal.

One feature of the freight traffic in the Exeter area was the local freight trip pilot, usually worked by one of the Laira-allocated Class 08s outbased at Exeter. The trip was centred on Exeter Riverside Yard but made visits to Exeter Central, Exmouth Junction and City Basin during the day. At Exmouth Junction was a carriage and wagon workshop and a coal concentration depot operated by Western Fuel. On 11 March 1983 the local trip is seen at Exeter Central, on return from Exmouth Junction, behind No. 08941 with a selection of repaired wagons.

Class 50s had been cascaded to the Waterloo to Exeter route once HSTs had taken over services from Paddington. When the more powerful Class 50s had taken over, the service was accelerated, but as the trains often called at most stations between Salisbury and Exeter the journey still took more than three hours and twenty minutes. The 1985 timetable saw eight through trains from Waterloo to Exeter as well as a number of short distance workings. The first arrival of the day at Exeter in the Down direction was 2V54, the 06.09 Salisbury to Exeter St Davids, seen arriving at Exeter Central behind No. 50048 *Dauntless* on 17 July 1985.

In 1908 the Exmouth branch had been doubled from Exmouth Junction as far as Topsham, but had been singled again in 1973 when Topsham became a passing loop – the only one on the branch. The 16.14 Exmouth to Exeter Central service departs Topsham on 11 March 1983 formed by Class 118 BRCW-built set P464, formed of vehicles Nos 51306, 59473 and 51321. Lifting barriers had been installed here in 1973, and the signal box closed in 1988 when control passed to Exmouth Junction signal box.

The Exmouth branch is the busiest branch in Devon and Cornwall: from 1981 the train service had settled at twenty-three trains each way on weekdays. There were eleven trains each way on Sunday, though there had been a spell in the 1970s where the branch was closed on Sundays during the winter. On 11 July 1984 the 14.11 service from Exeter St Davids approaches Exmouth and is passing the site of the former junction of the branch to Budleigh Salterton and Tipton St John. Set P469 is formed of vehicles Nos 51311, 59480 and 51326.

In the early 1960s the West of England had received a number of Class 121 Pressed Steel single power cars for work on lightly used lines. In 1985 they were replaced by Class 142 railbus sets. In 1987, with the Class 142 sets deemed unsuitable, six Gloucester-built Class 122 single power cars were sent as replacement. Laira received vehicles Nos 55000, 55003, 55005, 55006, 55009 and 55012. At Exmouth, No. 55003 (set P103) is seen in company with another member of the class on 13 July 1988.

At the height of the summer, Saturday timetable trains would be passing along the South Devon coast at ten-minute intervals, many of them loco-hauled services. Class 50 No. 50016 *Barham* was one of over twenty members of the class to pass during the day on 11 August 1984. The train is 1V76, the 09.36 Liverpool Lime Street to Penzance. In the distance, light engine No. 47490 heads towards Exeter.

One of the Cardiff Canton-based named Class 47s, No. 47087 *Cyclops,* passes through Dawlish Warren on 13 August 1983 with a motorail service. The train is 1C14, the 07.30 Paddington to St Austell service. This train also called at Newton Abbot to detach motorail flats. On the Up platform the Dawlish Warren Railway Museum occupied the station building from 1974 to 1984.

A camping coach had been first stationed in the goods yard at Dawlish Warren in the 1930s by the GWR. Camping coaches were then re-introduced after the war and became a well-known feature of Dawlish Warren. On 30 June 1984, 1V64, 07.17 Derby to Penzance, passes on the Down main behind No. 45129 of Toton depot.

Although Class 33s had been a regular sight in parts of the West Country, the appearance of one on a summer Saturday working to Paignton was unusual. On 30 June 1984, Eastleigh-allocated No. 33008 *Eastleigh* worked 1C18, the 08.36 Cardiff Central to Paignton service, and is seen here departing Dawlish Warren with some enthusiastic passengers.

Although the majority of summer Saturday services on the cross-country route were worked by locos and coaches, a few trains were formed by HST sets. Passing Dawlish Warren on 30 June 1984 is a HST forming 1M85, the 11.10 Paignton to Manchester Piccadilly service. Dawlish Warren was mostly served by the sparse local train service supplemented by a couple of the services from Paddington on summer Saturdays.

From the popular vantage point of Langstone Rock there is a good view of Dawlish Warren. On 13 August 1983 Laira-allocated No. 50009 *Conqueror* rounds the curve towards Dawlish with the 09.20 Brighton to Plymouth. No. 50009 had taken over the train at Exeter St Davids.

Many locos not fitted with train heating equipment were used on summer Saturdays to work the additional services. On 30 June 1984 Crewe diesel depot's No. 47322 headed west. The service is 1V71, the 08.22 Liverpool Lime Street to Paignton, which is seen approaching Dawlish.

By the 1980s the signal box at Dawlish was only manned on summer Saturdays, being generally switched out of use. On 30 June 1984 Toton-allocated No. 45105 passes the Up starting signal at Dawlish with a train for the west. The signal box eventually closed for good in September 1986, and Exeter panel signal box subsequently extended its area of coverage down to Newton Abbot in November 1986.

1V83, the 10.39 Manchester Piccadilly to Paignton cross-country HST service, is seen at Dawlish on 30 June 1984. The train is standing on the viaduct over Dawlish Water, where black swans have been resident since 1906, having been introduced from New Zealand by a Dawlish-born man. Although some summer Saturday trains ran non-stop from Exeter to Newton Abbot, there were seventeen west-bound trains that called at Dawlish and Teignmouth between 11.00 and 17.00.

On Saturday 3 July 1982 an unidentified Class 45 Peak rounds the curve towards Teignmouth, heading west. The following week strike action started, in a dispute over flexible rostering for drivers.

Commencing in late 1981, HSTs were introduced onto the cross-country network. The fleet comprised eighteen sets each formed with seven coaches. Running into the Down platform at Teignmouth on 3 July 1982 is a cross-country HST forming the 07.30 Newcastle to Paignton service.

Heading up the Teign Estuary at Teignmouth in the late afternoon of 21 July 1984 is No. 50049 *Defiance,* one of the Class 50 allocation to Laira. The train is 1V86, the 13.44 Birmingham New Street to Paignton service.

The train service on the Newquay branch varied greatly during the year, with extra services running in the summer, particularly on Saturdays. On Saturday 3 July 1982 No. 50013 *Agincourt* passes on the Up through line at Newton Abbot with the 10.45 Newquay to Paddington service. No. 50042 *Triumph* stands on the bay line formerly used by Moretonhampstead branch trains. As Newton Abbot depot had closed the previous year, it is possible that No. 50042 was acting as a standby loco in the event of a failure.

Prior to the re-signalling in 1987 there were four platform roads at Newton Abbot arranged on each side of a pair of island platforms, and in addition there were two through lines. On Saturday 3 July 1982 Crewe diesel depot's No. 47266 calls at Platform 3 on the Up relief line.

Newton Abbot was a railway town and a small loco depot had been built adjacent to the station by the South Devon Railway soon after the line opened. In 1892 a workshop and larger depot was opened. From 1962 diesel maintenance was carried out, but after 1970 only fuelling and servicing took place. On 21 July 1980 three locos, Nos 45044 *Royal Inniskilling Fusilier*, 50010 *Monarch* and 47531, stand in the 1962-built servicing shed. Nos 25058 and 45054 are stabled in the roofless remains of the 1892 loco shed, to the right. The depot finally closed in 1981.

On Saturday 20 July 1985 a Paddington-bound HST with power car No. 43035 on the rear calls at Newton Abbot. These two lines, the Up through line and the Up main line, were both removed in the 1987 re-signalling of Newton Abbot. This allowed step-free access from the station front to the platform.

One of the Bath Road ETH-fitted Class 31/4s, No. 31424, departs Newton Abbot with the 11.28 service to Paignton on 5 November 1981. In 1987 the track layout here was heavily rationalised during the re-signalling works; the three through platform lines in this photo remained, but everything else to the right of the train was removed.

Toton-allocated No. 45104 enters Newton Abbot on the Up relief line and passes Newton Abbot West signal box with the 15.04 Paignton to Birmingham New Street on 20 July 1985. In the background are the offices of book publishers David & Charles and part of the former South Devon Railway wagon works.

Beyond Newton Abbot is a four-track section to Aller Junction, where the Paignton line diverges. On Saturday 9 July 1983 Toton depot's No. 45056 is running on the down main line approaching Aller Junction. The loco is one of Toton's boiler-isolated Class 45s. It was normally restricted to freight work during the winter but was sometimes used on passenger turns during the summer timetable.

Seen at Aller Junction on Saturday 9 July 1983 is a train for Paignton running on the Down relief line. The loco is one of the Stratford-allocated silver-roof Class 47s, No. 47114. This was another loco with an isolated train heating boiler.

A Paddington-bound service passes Aller Junction signal box on 9 July 1983 behind No. 50031 *Hood,* having just descended Dainton Bank, which is one of the steepest main line gradients on the network. Aller Junction signal box would close in May 1987 as part of Stage 6 of the Exeter re-signalling scheme.

On summer Saturdays there were few local stopping services along the South Devon main line and DMU workings were mostly confined to early morning and late afternoon services. One of Laira Depot's thirteen BRCW-built Class 118 sets stands at Paignton on the evening of Saturday 31 July 1982. Set P471, formed of vehicles Nos 51314, 59481 and 51329, will work the 18.15 service to Exeter St Davids.

Most of the summer Saturday services that terminated at Paignton went empty stock to Goodrington carriage sidings, to run round and await their time until working back. On 31 July 1982 No. 50029 *Renown* passes Paignton South signal box with empty stock for Goodrington. When the Paignton area was re-signalled in 1988 the signal box survived as a gate box controlling the level crossings at each end of Paignton station.

At Plymouth on 15 April 1983, No. 47477 of Landore depot departs with the 07.40 Penzance to Liverpool Lime Street service. It is seen passing the former North Road East signal box, which had closed in 1960 when the new Plymouth panel signal box opened. In the platform, No. 50032 *Courageous* waits with empty stock for Laira.

Laira depot first received an allocation of Class 25s in 1971 when ten members of the class were transferred as replacements for the last surviving Class 22 diesel-hydraulics. In October 1971 No. 25223 was one of the locos allocated to Laira. It was to remain based there for the rest of its working life, being withdrawn in October 1980. On 22 September 1980, just weeks before withdrawal, No. 25223 is seen on jacks at Laira depot.

In 1982 Laira depot had an allocation of thirteen Class 08s for shunting and local freight trip work. There were normally three or four of the allocation outbased at Exeter and one at Meldon Quarry, while the remainder worked in the Plymouth area. The Plymouth station pilot duty was being covered by No. 08895, which is seen in the parcels bay platform on 21 April 1982.

Speedlink services to and from St Blazey called at Tavistock Junction Yard to attach and detach traffic to and from various freight locations in Plymouth. Three local freight trips were based on the yard, each worked by a Laira Class 08. One of these worked to Keyham, Devonport Dockyard and Ernesettle MOD. On 15 November 1982 No. 08953 is crossing Pennycomequick Viaduct on the return trip to Tavistock Junction. The VEAs have come from Ernesettle MOD depot probably containing dangerous goods, with the former BR ferry van acting as a barrier wagon.

On 15 April 1983 a HST set forming the 10.20 Penzance to Newcastle cross-country service calls at Bodmin Road. The station is located in a rural location in the Fowey Valley and is over 3 miles from the town of Bodmin. On 4 November 1983 the station was renamed Bodmin Parkway.

Cornwall is famous for its produce and for many years there had been a lunchtime departure from Penzance referred to in the working timetable (WTT) as a 'perishables and parcels' service. By 1983 the train had become 3S15, the 12.10 Penzance to Glasgow Salkeld Street parcels. It is seen climbing up to Bodmin Road on 15 April 1983 behind No. 47512, an Old Oak Common loco. This train was often heavily loaded and the WTT showed the train was permitted to load up to 525 tons.

When Laira had lost its allocation of Class 25s in 1980 a number of class 37s were transferred in as replacements, and in 1983 there were five allocated to Laira. One of the five, No. 37181, approaches Bodmin Road with empty clayhoods for Wenford Bridge on 14 April 1983. Class 37s were not permitted to run to Wenford Bridge so the empties will be taken up for loading by a local trip worked by one of the St Blazey Class 08 shunting locos.

Far from home, Gateshead depot's No. 47402 *Gateshead* departs from Lostwithiel with the 11.05 Penzance to Plymouth service on 15 November 1982. Milk had been an important feature of traffic from the West Country for many decades but regular traffic ceased in 1980. The milk tanks seen in the Unigate sidings at Lostwithiel had been refurbished in 1981 by the Milk Marketing Board for use in an emergency, but they saw very little use.

As well as the long-distance services, there were also three or four loco-hauled trains each way between Plymouth and Penzance formed of short sets of Mark 1 coaching stock. Some of these services were also booked to convey parcels vans on the rear. Approaching the level crossing at Lostwithiel on 23 June 1982 is the 13.50 Plymouth to Penzance service hauled by No. 50040 *Leviathan,* which was one of the Old Oak Common allocation.

During a spell of Cornish liquid sunshine, No. 37274 runs through Lostwithiel with loaded clayhoods of export clay for Fowey on 23 June 1982. The train would run round in the loop at the other end of the station before heading down the branch to Fowey. China clay came from a number of locations in Cornwall including Drinnick Mill, Parkandillack, Burngullow, Goonbarrow, Wenford Bridge and Moorswater. Export clay traffic also came from loading points in Devon, at Marsh Mills, Heathfield and sometimes from North Devon.

The driver of No. 47402 *Gateshead,* working the 13.50 Plymouth to Penzance service, waits for station work to be completed at Par on 15 November 1982. Par is the junction for the Newquay branch but it was poorly served, with only seven trains each way on weekdays. Passengers for the branch train will have a thirty-minute wait until the 14.45 departure for Newquay.

On 16 July 1980 a Class 119 Gloucester-built DMU arrives at Par with the 12.35 service from Newquay. Set C593 was a Cardiff Canton-based set formed of vehicles Nos 51072, 59431 and 51085. In the distance is DMU No. 55026 (set P126), which had been used to strengthen services on the branch earlier in the day.

The hub of the freight network in Cornwall was at St Blazey. The depot there had an allocation of three Class 08 shunting locos, while several of the Laira-allocated Class 37s were also outbased there to work local freight trips. In this view on 16 July 1980 the yard pilot is St Blazey's No. 08954, and various clay wagons are stabled in the yard. The signal box stands adjacent to St Blazey station, which had closed as long ago as 1925. On the right is a rake of air-braked vans.

When the Class 50 refurbishment programme at Doncaster Works commenced in the late 1970s the first six members of the class to be completed were outshopped in rail blue livery. These included No. 50001 *Dreadnought,* which was released to traffic on 9 April 1980. Three years later, on 8 March 1983, No. 50001 *Dreadnought* is still in rail blue livery when seen at St Austell working the 09.20 Liverpool Lime Street to Penzance service.

One of the six Class 50s to be released after refurbishment at Doncaster Works, still in rail blue livery, was No. 50047 *Swiftsure*. It is seen calling at St Austell on 15 April 1983 with 1Z95, the 14.48 Penzance to Paddington, which was a relief service to the 15.00 Penzance to Paddington.

A general view of St Austell station on 8 March 1983 as the 15.00 Penzance to Paddington HST service calls. To the left of the station are the sidings of St Austell Motorail terminal. The Motorail service was seasonal, running from May to September each year. It last ran to St Austell during the summer of 1984.

One of the loco-hauled services in the West Country was 1B59, the 13.45 Penzance to Bristol Temple Meads, seen here arriving at St Austell on 15 April 1983 behind No. 45137 *The Bedfordshire and Hertfordshire Regiment T.A.* This service was booked to convey parcel vans on the rear and was consequently allowed plenty of time at various stations stops, including five minutes at Camborne, Truro and St Austell. It also waited for fifteen minutes at Plymouth.

By 1983 most Peak locos had received panelled-over nose fronts, and only a few Class 45s, including No. 45128, still retained their headcode panels. On 8 March 1983 No. 45128 is seen at Truro with 2B12, the 10.22 Plymouth to Penzance service. This train was formed out of the 06.35 Bristol Temple Meads to Plymouth service, which also conveyed mail and parcels, so additional station time was allowed for unloading at many stops.

Penwithers Junction to the west of Truro is where the Falmouth Branch diverges from the Cornish main line. On 8 March 1983 the 08.25 Paddington to Penzance HST service crosses the junction. In the distance BRCW-built Class 118 DMU set P465, formed of vehicles Nos 51307, 59474 and 51322, waits to come off the branch with the 12.30 Falmouth to Truro service. From 1852 to 1855 there had been a station here known as Truro Road, which built by the West Cornwall Railway.